STECK-VAUGHN

PORTRAIT OF AMERICA

Utah

Steck-Vaughn Company

Executive Editor	Diane Sharpe
Senior Editor	Martin S. Saiewitz
Design Manager	Pamela Heaney
Photo Editor	Margie Foster
Electronic Cover Graphics	Alan Klemp

Proof Positive/Farrowlyne Associates, Inc.
Program Editorial, Revision Development, Design, and Production

Consultant: Utah State Historical Society

Published by Raintree Steck-Vaughn Publishers, an imprint of Steck-Vaughn Company.

A Turner Educational Services, Inc. book. Based on the Portrait of America television series by R. E. (Ted) Turner.

Cover Photo: Canyonlands National Park by © Scott Melcer.

Library of Congress Cataloging-in-Publication Data

Thompson, Kathleen.
    Utah / Kathleen Thompson.
      p. cm. — (Portrait of America)
    "Based on the Portrait of America television series" — T.p. verso.
    "A Turner book."
    Includes index.
    ISBN 0-8114-7390-2 (library binding). — ISBN 0-8114-7471-2 (softcover)
    1. Utah—Juvenile literature. [1. Utah.] I. Portrait of
America (Television program) II. Title. III. Series: Thompson,
Kathleen. Portrait of America.
F826.3.T46 1996
979—dc20

                                      95-50426
                                         CIP
                                         AC

Printed and Bound in the United States of America

1 2 3 4 5 6 7 8 9 10 WZ 98 97 96 95

Acknowledgments
The publishers wish to thank the following for permission to reproduce photographs:
P. 7 © Scott Melcer; p. 8 © Kevin O. Mooney/Odyssey; p. 10 © Scott Melcer; pp. 11 (both), 12, 13, 14 Utah State Historical Society; p. 15 (top) Utah State Historical Society, (bottom) © The Church of Jesus Christ of Latter-day Saints, Used by permission; p. 16 John Yesco; p. 17 Golden Spike National Historic Site, National Park Service; p. 19 © Gayla Carpenter/U.S. Bureau of Reclamation; p. 20 © John DeVillbiss/Utah State University Extension; p. 21 Utah State Historical Society; p. 22 Novell, Inc.; p. 24 Kennecott; p. 25 (top) Utah State University Extension, (bottom) E Sytems, Montek Division; p. 26 (both) © John DeVillbiss/Utah State University Extension; p. 27 Utah Travel Promotion; pp. 28, 29 (both) © The Church of Jesus Christ of Latter-day Saints, Used by permission; p. 30 © Superstock; p. 32 © Scott Melcer; p. 33 Special Collections & Archives, Utah State University; p. 34 Utah State Historical Society; p. 35 (top) Utah State Historical Society, (bottom) © The Church of Jesus Christ of Latter-day Saints, Used by permission; pp. 36, 37 Utah Travel Promotion; p. 38 Utah Symphony; p. 39 Vanguard Media; p. 40 © Tom Dietrich/Tony Stone Images; pp. 41, 42 © Scott Melcer; p. 44 Salt Lake City Convention & Visitors Bureau; p. 46 One Mile Up; p. 47 (left) One Mile Up, (center) © William D. Bransford/National Wildflower Research Center, (right) © A. Cruickshank/Vireo.

STECK-VAUGHN

PORTRAIT OF AMERICA

Utah

Kathleen Thompson

A Turner Book

RSVP

RAINTREE
STECK-VAUGHN
PUBLISHERS

The Steck-Vaughn Company

Austin, Texas

Bear Lake

Logan

Brigham City

Ogden

GREAT SALT LAKE DESERT

Great Salt Lake

▲ Kings Peak

☆ **SALT LAKE CITY**

Tooele

Vernal

Orem

Provo

Utah Lake

DINOS NATIO MONU

ROCKY MOUNTAINS

Price

Green River

Richfield

Moab

Monroe

CANYONLANDS NATIONAL PARK

CAPITOL REEF NATIONAL PARK

Milford

Colorado River

Cedar City

BRYCE CANYON NATIONAL PARK

Saint George

Lake Powell

San Juan River

Utah

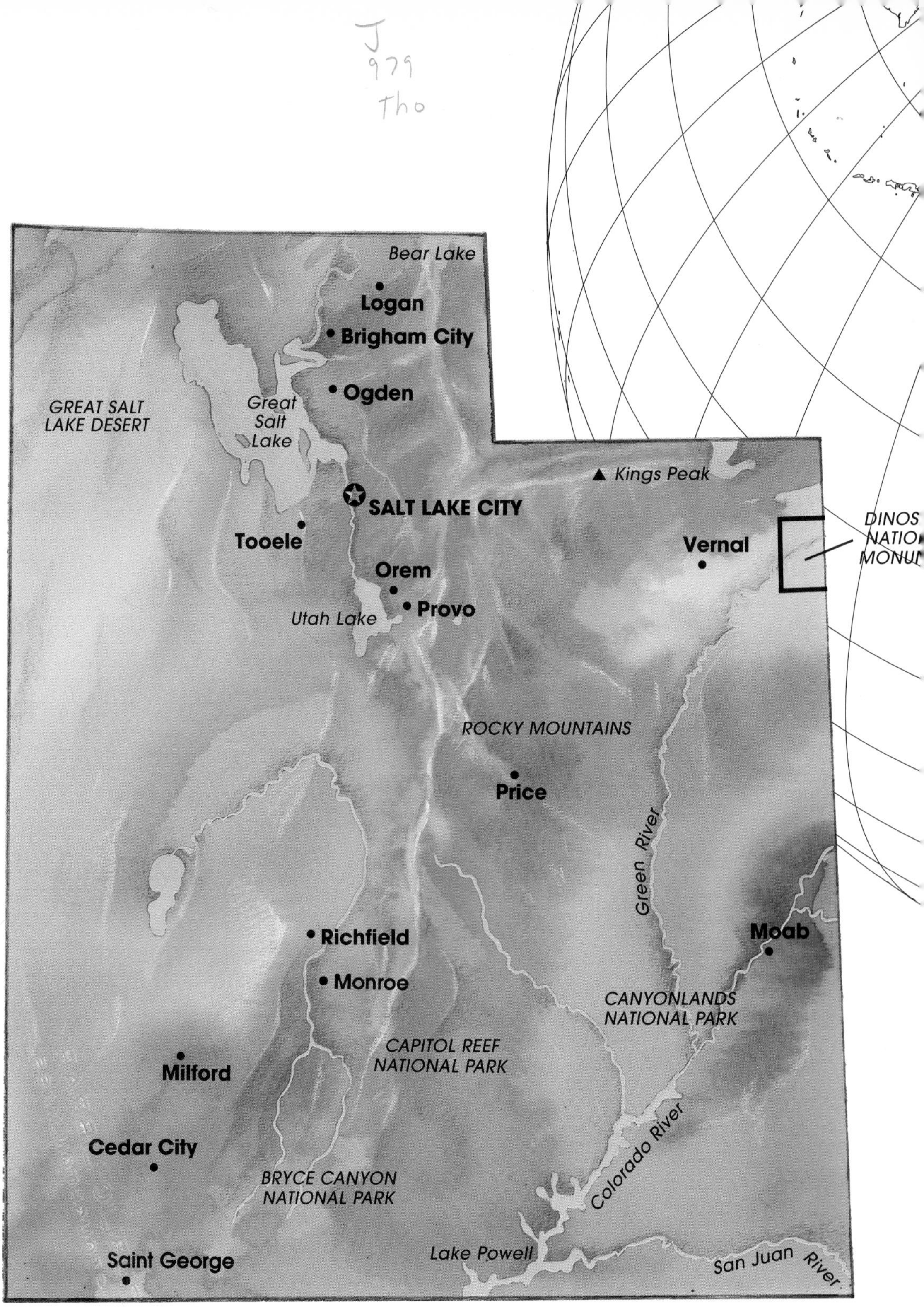

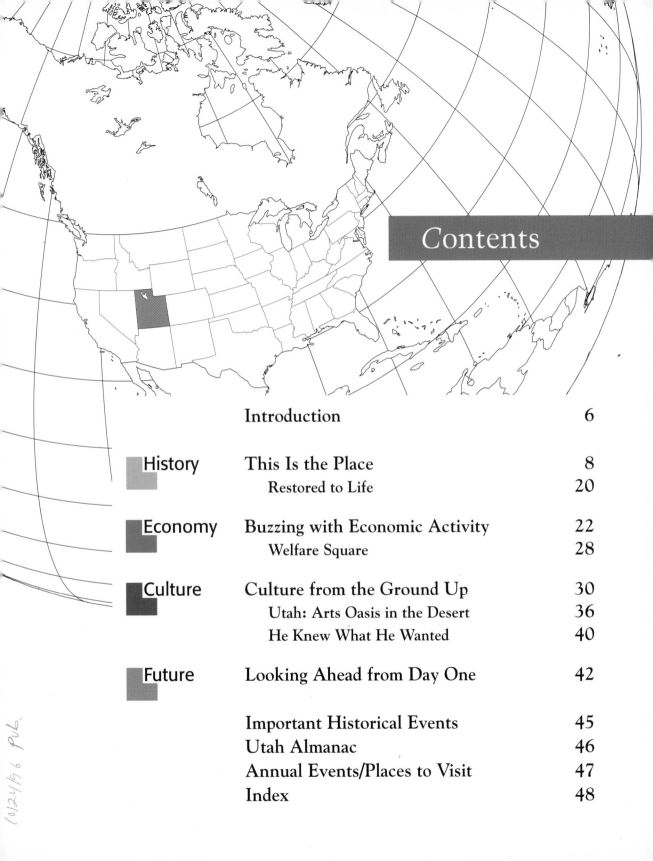

Contents

Introduction

The explorer John C. Frémont charted the land now called Utah in the nineteenth century. It is hard to imagine what he thought of when he descended the snowcapped Rocky Mountains and encountered the canyons of the Colorado Plateau. Rivers have cut this landscape into deep gorges, exposing rock layers varying in hues from white to red. Miles of rock towers have been twisted and carved by centuries of rain and wind. Frémont named the area west of the plateau the Great Basin. This area includes the remains of prehistoric Lake Bonneville, an inland sea now dried up. In its place lies a 14-mile expanse of salt desert packed hard as rock. The land Frémont explored has changed in some ways during the last century, but it remains unusual, majestic, and starkly beautiful.

Canyonlands National Park, which was carved by the Green and Colorado rivers, is Utah's largest national park.

Utah

This Is the Place

Utah's first inhabitants began arriving in present-day Utah about 12,000 years ago. These prehistoric Native Americans lived in caves along the edges of Lake Bonneville. They gathered roots, nuts, and berries and hunted animals such as antelope, mountain sheep, and rabbits. Parts of Lake Bonneville have since dried up, forming three smaller lakes—Great Salt Lake, Sevier Lake, and Utah Lake. Archaeologists believe that at one time, Lake Bonneville spread over thirty thousand square miles.

Around A.D. 400, Native Americans called the Anasazi settled in southern Utah. At first they lived in houses that they built into the ground. Later they developed huge apartment-like buildings made of rock and clay. The Anasazi were good farmers, and they developed advanced methods of irrigation.

Another Native American group, the Fremont, lived north of the Anasazi settlements around 900. They also lived in houses built into the ground. They raised squash, corn, and beans and gathered nuts and

These spires at Bryce Canyon National Park were formed by more than sixty million years of wind and water erosion.

9

Ancient Native American drawings such as these are called *petroglyphs,* which means "rock drawings."

roots from the forest. The Fremont were also excellent potters.

Sometime around 1300, however, both the Anasazi and the Fremont broke up into smaller groups. By the early 1700s, there were five main Native American groups living in present-day Utah: the Paiute in the southwestern region, the Gosiute in the western deserts, the Shoshone in the northwest, the Ute in the eastern area, and the Navajo in the southeastern corner.

The first Europeans to visit the Utah area were two Spanish priests who traveled north from Mexico: Francisco Atanasio Domínguez and Silvestre Vélez de Escalante. They reached the north-central Utah area in 1776. In the course of their explorations, the two priests cleared a path for future traders and explorers.

Another 75 years passed before there was any other outside interest in present-day Utah. Then the area was visited mostly by rugged trappers called mountain men, who roamed throughout the Rocky Mountains. The mountain men were hired by various fur-trading companies to obtain the furs of small animals. They sold their furs at an annual gathering called a *rendezvous*, where they also bought supplies for the coming year. James Bridger was one of the first of these mountain men. In 1824 Bridger became the first non-Native American to see the Great Salt Lake.

The mountain men left the Rocky Mountains around 1840 when the number of fur-bearing animals

This historic photograph shows members of the Ute, the Native Americans for whom the state of Utah is named.

declined. In 1842 the United States government sent John C. Frémont to make maps of the uncharted territory between the Rocky Mountains and California. Frémont's travels took him through present-day Utah, from the mountain region to the dry western area that he named the Great Basin.

In 1847 a group of people called the Mormons arrived in the area. Their arrival had a profound effect on the history of Utah. Seventeen years earlier, Joseph Smith had founded the Church of Jesus Christ of Latter-day Saints in Fayette, New York. The Mormons, as they were called, often had financial troubles as well as conflicts with other religions. Smith moved the congregation often. He took them from New York to Ohio to Missouri and finally to Nauvoo, Illinois, in 1844.

By this time, the Mormon congregation numbered about 35,000 members, and Joseph Smith was at the peak of his power. Some of his religious and political views angered a number of people at Nauvoo, however. Smith and his brother were arrested, and later they

At age 14 Joseph Smith claimed that God and Jesus Christ appeared to him and told him not to join any of the existing churches. Smith founded the Church of Jesus Christ of Latter-day Saints, also known as the Mormon church.

Brigham Young became the second leader of the Mormon church. In its early years, the church allowed the practice of polygamy, so Young had almost thirty wives and more than fifty children in his lifetime.

were killed in a mob attack. Brigham Young became the leader of the Mormon church after Smith's death. He decided to lead an advance group of 148 people to find a new settlement in the West. His goal was to find a place where the Mormons could practice their religion in their own community. When the group at last reached Great Salt Lake in present-day Utah in 1847, he knew the Mormons' search had ended. "This is the place," he supposedly said. The pioneer party set to work planting crops and building a new settlement.

The Mormon settlement grew rapidly as the congregation recruited new members. Most of the new members arrived from the eastern United States, but others were from Scandinavia and Great Britain.

One year earlier, the United States and Mexico had gone to war over a border dispute. In 1848 the two countries signed the Treaty of Guadalupe Hidalgo, concluding the war. The treaty granted much of the West, including what is now Utah, to the United States. In 1849 the Mormons petitioned the United States government for statehood. They proposed to name their settlement the State of Deseret. One year later, the federal government accepted the settlement as a territory instead, renaming it the Utah Territory.

The arrival of so many settlers in the Territory angered the Native Americans living there. The

Native Americans were forced to share much of the land and the hunting with the settlers. A Ute chief named Wakara, whom the settlers called Walker, began leading raids on the Mormon settlements in 1853. The raids only lasted about a year because Brigham Young met with Walker and persuaded him to stop the raids. Relations between the Mormons and the Ute continued peacefully for about ten more years.

Meanwhile, the Utah Territory continued to apply for statehood. Congress refused the applications many times. Part of the reason Congress was reluctant to make Utah Territory a state was that Mormons made up such a large percentage of the population. The Mormon religion was not common outside of the Territory, and Congress was uncomfortable allowing one group to control an entire state. Another reason was that the Mormon church practiced polygamy. Polygamy is the marriage of one person to more than one mate at the same time. Not more than ten percent of Mormon husbands actually had more than one wife,

This historic photo shows St. George, one of Utah's early Mormon settlements. The winter home of Brigham Young is now a tourist attraction there.

but many people across the nation were shocked that the Mormon church allowed the practice at all.

Rumors started that the Mormons were attempting to rebel against the United States. President James Buchanan acted on these rumors without investigation. In 1857 he sent more than two thousand armed soldiers to Utah to prevent this supposed rebellion. The Mormons became fearful that the army was coming to drive them from their homes. A wagon train of settlers from Arkansas happened to be passing through Utah Territory at the time. Some Mormons believed these settlers were responsible for the murder of founder Joseph Smith 13 years earlier. They refused to sell food to these travelers, and angry words were exchanged. Finally, a small group of Mormons joined local Native Americans in attacking the wagon train. Almost all of the 140 innocent settlers were killed.

As soldiers neared Utah in the spring of 1858, Brigham Young ordered all of the residents of Salt Lake City to leave their homes and move south to avoid a

These federal troops were sent to end a nonexistent Mormon rebellion in the Mormon War of 1858.

battle. A few stayed behind to set fire to the city if they saw soldiers approaching. Talks of compromise began before any fires were lit, however. Brigham Young agreed to step down as governor of the Territory. Although the episode came to be called the Utah War, or the Mormon War, no battle ever took place.

In 1862 the federal government outlawed the practice of polygamy. President Abraham Lincoln sent troops to Salt Lake City to guard the transportation routes. While there, Colonel Patrick Connor encouraged his troops to prospect for minerals. He sought to start a mining boom in the Territory, which would bring more non-Mormons. The plan worked to some degree as mining companies established themselves in the area over the next decade.

above. The Mormon Temple, shown here under construction, took forty years to complete, from 1853 to 1893. The dome-shaped Tabernacle is to its left.

below. Salt Lake City's Mormon Temple cost about four million dollars to build.

The federal government began a policy in 1864 to force the Ute to live on a reservation, an area of land set aside for them. A Ute leader named Black Hawk began raiding settlers in central Utah Territory to protest this federal policy. These raids were the beginning of what later became known as the Black Hawk War. Warriors from many Native American groups joined Black Hawk in these raids. By 1868, however, most of the

Ute were forced to move to the reservation in north-eastern Utah Territory.

In the meantime, inventions were beginning to change the nation. In 1861 the first cross-country telegraph line, stretching from California to Washington, D.C., had been completed in Salt Lake City. One year later, the federal government passed the Pacific Railroad Act. The act was the first step in building a railroad system that would stretch unbroken across the United States. The Central Pacific began laying track eastward from Sacramento, California, in 1863. Two years later, the Union Pacific Railroad began building west from Omaha, Nebraska. The two branches of the nation's first transcontinental railroad were joined at Promontory, Utah, in 1869. The new transcontinental railroad system shortened the travel time between the coasts from three months to eight days.

In 1879 the United States Supreme Court upheld the law against polygamy. Federal officers were sent to Utah to arrest anyone who continued to practice it. About 12,000 Mormon polygamists were refused the

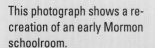
This photograph shows a re-creation of an early Mormon schoolroom.

This photograph shows the meeting of the two branches of the nation's first transcontinental railroad. The last spike—made of gold—was driven in at Promontory in 1869.

right to hold office and to vote. About 1,300 were jailed. Then in 1887 the Edmunds-Tucker Act took away the property of the Mormon church. Three years later, the Mormons gave up the practice of polygamy. Utah applied for statehood for the seventh time and was finally admitted as the forty-fifth state in 1896.

The beginning of a new century brought many exciting events to Utah. Increased irrigation, along with the introduction of dry-farming methods, opened up new farmland. The discovery of valuable minerals, such as copper, silver, lead, and coal, boosted the state's economy. Railroads connected Utah with the rest of the nation. When the United States entered World War I in 1917, farms and factories needed to increase their production for the war effort. Utah's farms and ranches provided food for soldiers. Utah's mines also experienced a boom as the United States bought metals to make war materials.

The end of the war in 1918 brought a decreased demand for these products. Utah's mines went into a decline, which continued into the 1920s. In the 1930s the entire nation fell into an economic slump called the Great Depression. Millions of people were out of work. Factories and banks closed. Utah was devastated.

Utah recovered with the rest of the nation in the late 1930s. It was mainly World War II, however, that brought Utah and the country back to economic health. The United States entered the war in 1941 when Japanese forces bombed Pearl Harbor, a United States Navy base in Hawaii. During the war, many weapons production plants and air bases were built in Utah. The government became the state's biggest employer, with more than one hundred thousand residents recruited for military construction.

In 1942 the federal government directed all people of Japanese descent living on the West Coast to move to internment camps. The government was fearful that any person of Japanese descent—even a citizen or a legal alien—might be a spy. More than eight thousand Japanese Americans were forced to live at Topaz camp in Utah's Millard County from 1942 to 1945. Many of these people lost their property, jobs, and possessions while they were kept at the camp.

After World War II ended in 1945, Utah's factories continued to make weapons, especially missiles.

Utah's economy also got a boost when uranium was discovered in the state in 1952. The federal government became the main consumer of uranium, buying large amounts for use in atomic weapons.

Beginning in the 1950s, Utah became increasingly concerned about environmental and conservation issues. In 1953 the state passed the Water Pollution Control Act to help maintain the quality of the state's water supply. Then in 1967 the state began work on the Central Utah Project. This was an irrigation and damming program designed to ensure enough water for the state's urban areas well into the twenty-first century.

The Utah government in the 1980s and early 1990s concentrated on attracting new industries—and therefore more residents—by loosening its tax laws and other corporate restrictions. Today, the state's unemployment rate is one of the lowest in the country.

Utah's population boom has also brought problems. One of the biggest arguments in Utah's state legislature is over how to use the land. New residents and businesses need to expand into areas that are not currently occupied. Many people in Utah do not want this expansion to reach into certain parts of the state. They want to protect as much of Utah's natural beauty as possible. The method by which Utah settles this issue could become a model for other states in the future.

The Jordanelle Dam is one of the dams built as part of the Central Utah Project. The Jordanelle Dam construction began in 1987.

Restored to Life

Before settlers began arriving in central Utah, the Paiute were self-sufficient and content. They hunted small game and harvested crops. They made baskets from grass, reeds, and willow rushes. Then settlers began to take over their land. Many Paiute died of European diseases such as cholera, tuberculosis, measles, and scarlet fever. Some Paiute groups lost as many as ninety percent of their members.

"Well, [at] one time, the Paiute owned all this land, everything," said a current member of the group. "When the federal government came to help my people, they put them on reservations. They gave them certain sections of land. And then they terminated [government recognition of] our tribe in 1954." In this case, the federal government stopped providing food and education for the group. The idea was to make the Paiute more self-reliant.

No one helped the Paiute adapt to their new independence, however. The effects on the group were destructive. The government no longer provided

The Paiute Restoration Gathering and Pow-wow is a festive event that includes dancing, drumming, and softball. This Paiute woman is dressed for dancing.

educators, so Paiute children grew up without going to school. Doctors were no longer available, so people who were too sick to travel to the nearest town stayed sick; or they died.

In addition, no one told the Paiute that the termination meant they would have to pay taxes on their land. As a result, the Paiute did not pay any taxes for years. Because the Paiute could not pay, the federal government took approximately 15,000 acres of their land. After lengthy legal struggles, the five hundred remaining members of the Utah Paiute at last gained back their federal recognition in 1980; the termination had ended.

The Paiute had lost a lot more than land and money between 1954 and 1980, however. Their extreme poverty had prevented them from holding most of their traditional celebrations. Less than half of them spoke the Paiute language. Traditional crafts, such as leather tanning, storytelling, and basket weaving, had almost disappeared.

So in 1981, the Utah Paiute held their first annual Restoration Gathering and Pow-wow. The purpose of the celebration, as a participant explained, is "to [bring back] some pride in the younger people and show our older people that we want to learn [the Paiute tradition]." In a sense, the Paiute are looking backward. But they are looking backward to a proud past that is important to the pride of their group. They are using that past to give themselves and their children a firm identity.

This nineteenth-century photograph shows a Paiute family in Utah.

Buzzing with Economic Activity

When the Mormons first came to Utah, they built a self-sufficient economy. What they needed, they made, grew, or raised. Utah's economy is still based on the ideals of hard work and self-sufficiency. These ideals have helped Utah become one of the nation's most economically successful states.

It is manufacturing that has given Utah's economy its strong position. Utah's manufacturing industry still averages about five thousand new jobs each year. In all, just over one hundred thousand Utah citizens work in manufacturing.

Transportation equipment is Utah's number-one manufacturing industry. Most workers in this industry make airplane parts. They also produce parts for missiles and rockets. Many of these companies have been in Utah since the 1950s, but some, such as the aircraft manufacturer McDonnell-Douglas, moved to the state in the 1980s.

The second most important area of manufacturing in Utah is food processing. When food is processed, it is

Industries rely on Utah's well-educated workforce as they expand their production of advanced technology. This woman is a software technician at Novell.

Although there was a devastating decline in the copper industry in the early 1980s, modernization helped copper mines to regain their importance in the later part of the decade. This photograph shows an open-pit copper mine near Salt Lake City.

cooked or changed in some other way, packaged, and sent to market. Canned or frozen corn, for example, is a processed food. Most of the canning and packaging plants in Utah are found in Salt Lake City and in areas north of the city. Dairy products are also an important part of Utah's food-processing industry.

One of the fastest-growing manufacturing industries in Utah is computer software. The industry began in the Provo and Orem area in 1979 when the software company WordPerfect was founded by a student and a professor at Brigham Young University. Almost two hundred companies have since followed their lead, giving the Provo/Orem area the nickname "Software Valley." These companies sell nearly $2.5 billion worth of products each year.

Another rapidly growing area of high-technology manufacturing in Utah is biomedical products, such as artificial hearts and limbs. Salt Lake City has recently attracted about 75 of these companies. Biomedical companies employ about eight thousand workers in Utah.

The most valuable product mined in Utah is oil. Next in importance is coal, which is mined mostly in the central part of the state. Utah is second only to Arizona in the nation's copper production. Gold, silver, natural gas, lead, and uranium are also mined. There are about 8,500 miners working in Utah. When the demand for mineral products declined in the early 1980s, almost ten thousand miners—about half of the miners in the state—lost their jobs. With the state government's help, most of these workers were retrained to work in the state's factories.

Another economic area in Utah that is small but still important is agriculture. There are about 12,000 farms and ranches in the state. Most of these are small and family-run. As in most western states, livestock generates the largest agricultural income. In fact, about four fifths of all agricultural production in the state comes from livestock, especially beef cattle, dairy cattle, turkeys, and sheep. Even the state's crops center around its livestock industry. Hay, grown to feed Utah's livestock, is the state's leading crop. In addition, Utah is one of the top states for growing barley, pears, and cherries. Utah is called the Beehive State because nearly one and a half million pounds of honey are produced each year!

As important as all of these areas are to Utah's economy, service industries, taken as a whole, outrank them all. Service industries are areas of work that provide services to people instead of making a product. About eighty percent of Utah's workers are employed in some type of service job. In all, services earn well over five billion dollars in Utah each year.

The most important area of service industries in Utah is community, social, and personal services. Utah has more than two hundred thousand workers

Utah cattle ranches bring in a total of almost $400 million each year.

This worker is helping to construct a part for an airplane.

This pipe and others like it carry water throughout Utah's farmland. Without irrigation, farming here would not be possible.

Windmills like this one were built in the 1800s and early 1900s. This windmill uses the energy of the wind to pump water for cattle to drink. Other windmills use wind energy to grind grain or generate electricity.

employed in these businesses. They include doctors, nurses, car mechanics, lawyers, and engineers.

Another two hundred thousand or so of Utah's workers are employed in service industries involving retail and wholesale trade. People who work in wholesale trade sell larger amounts of items, such as produce and cars, to companies such as grocery stores and car dealerships.

The fastest-growing area of service industries in Utah is finance, insurance, and real estate. The number of businesses in this category grew by at least ten percent each year in the early 1990s. Workers in this category include bank tellers, insurance agents, and real estate agents.

About another 175,000 of Utah's workers are employed by federal, state, and local government. These workers include public schoolteachers, park rangers, and elected officials. The income of government workers totals about four billion dollars a year.

One major Utah service industry is the tourist industry. Visitors from across the country and the world come to hike, ski, bicycle, and raft in Utah.

The tourist industry also includes people who come to the state on business, especially to attend conventions. Visitors to Utah have turned tourism into a three billion dollar industry.

Utah's economy is thriving. Nationwide publications and reports have backed up this statement. One magazine reported that Utah led the nation in job creation in 1994. Another report placed Utah second in the nation in economic performance, business strength, and new development potential. Salt Lake City has been rated the most economically healthy city in the nation. But Utah citizens do not need these outside sources to assess the health of their state. The evidence is all around them.

Park City was once a silver mining boomtown, but the silver eventually ran out. It probably would have become a ghost town if it hadn't turned into a tourist spot especially popular with skiers.

Welfare Square

The Mormons have a unique way of referring to themselves in their religion. All members of the Mormon faith are considered part of a community. The goal of the community is to look out for each and every member. One way of doing this is through Welfare Square in Salt Lake City.

Welfare Square consists of a storehouse, a cannery, a bakery, a milk plant, and various administrative offices. It takes up an entire city block. It is staffed by about fifty regular employees and about two hundred volunteers, most of whom process and prepare food for needy church members.

Construction on Welfare Square began in 1938, toward the end of the Great Depression, one of the most difficult times in our nation's history. Millions of people across the nation were out of work during the Great Depression. Some people could not buy enough food to feed their family. Many people simply went hungry. The Mormon church struggled through the worst of these years, then decided to ensure that they would always be prepared to provide for their community members in need.

A few years ago, Gene and Maryanne Schmidt needed help when Gene unexpectedly lost his job. "We just didn't know when he was going to get a job or whether or not the bills would be paid," remembered Maryanne. But their church was ready to help. They provided the Schmidts with food and any household items and clothing that they couldn't afford.

They also provided Gene with a job at the Welfare Square butcher shop to keep him working until he

Utah's people give more money to charity than people in any other state in the country. Welfare Square is a product of their generosity.

Welfare Square and other Mormon welfare facilities throughout the United States find jobs for more than fifty thousand people every year.

could find another job. Many people don't like to feel that they are receiving handouts. But with Gene working at Welfare Square, he could see the food and supplies that the church provided him with as pay, not as handouts.

The generosity of Welfare Square isn't reserved for its own members. Much of the food processed and packaged there goes to worldwide relief efforts. Welfare Square also has a Transient Services office, where all people who are in need can volunteer their work in exchange for food, clothing, a place to sleep, or even a bus ticket home.

Welfare Square is a program that is based on love and the belief in human dignity. People of all faiths, and in every community, can learn from Welfare Square's practical and effective system of support for people in need.

Food from the Mormon Welfare Cannery helps people all around the world, not just in the United States.

Culture from the Ground Up

There was some earth-shaking activity going on in Utah long before any explorers or mountain men arrived there. It was happening even before Native Americans lived on the land. Tens of thousands of years ago, winged, walking, and swimming dinosaurs made present-day Utah their home. Dinosaur National Monument in Jensen has provided scientists and museums with more dinosaur bones than any other site in the world. Visitors can see skeletons on display and walk through an archaeological site where bones are still waiting to be unearthed. These prehistoric artifacts give scientists a clearer picture of what life was like before people populated the landscape.

The Utah Field House of Natural History State Park in Vernal also has fascinating exhibits of dinosaur skeletons and prehistoric artifacts. The exhibit in the Dinosaur Garden has full-sized dinosaur replicas on display. At the Earth Science Museum at Brigham Young University in Provo, visitors watch as paleontologists dig up and examine prehistoric artifacts.

Summer tourism is as important to Utah's economy as winter tourism. Rafting is especially popular on the Green River in the northeastern part of the state.

The spectacular landscape of Utah has a powerful influence on the culture of the state. This photo shows a scene from Bryce Canyon National Park.

Native Americans were the state's first artists. Archaeologists have found tools, fragments of pottery, and cave drawings made by various groups. Many of these artifacts are on display at Hovenweep National Monument and Anasazi Indian Village State Park in southern Utah. Some of these artifacts date back as early as the eleventh century. Artifacts belonging to the Fremont from as early as the tenth century are on display at Fremont Indian State Park near Sevier.

Perhaps the most well-known example of Utah's culture belongs to the days of the Wild West. One of Utah's best remembered figures from this era is Butch Cassidy. Born George Leroy Parker in Circleville in 1867, Cassidy became one of the most famous—and most wanted—outlaws of the West. He robbed trains and banks throughout the Rocky Mountains. In the 1890s, Cassidy became so well known he had trouble hiding from the law. He returned to Utah to hide out in the south-central section of the state, at what is known today as Capitol Reef National Park. In 1901 Cassidy escaped to New York and then South America. The rest of his life is unknown. Some stories say he was killed in South America. Others claim he returned to the United States and died in 1937.

Utah certainly has had its share of great writers. Many of them, such as Wallace Stegner, wrote about the state. Stegner spent much of his life studying and teaching at the University of Utah. In 1964 he published *The Gathering of Zion*, a historical book about the Mormons' long journey from Illinois to Utah in the 1840s. He is best known for his novel *Angle of Repose*, which won the Pulitzer Prize in 1972.

Critic and historian Bernard De Voto, born in Ogden in 1897, also drew on his experience in Utah and the rest of the West for his work. His book *Across the Wide Missouri* won the Pulitzer Prize in 1948.

Another Utah writer, poet May Swenson, was born in Logan in 1913 and graduated from Utah State University. One of her most interesting books is *Iconographs*, a collection of poems that are not set in standard lines of type. Instead, the lines form shapes or designs on the page that reflect the poems' content. Swenson won numerous fellowships and prizes and was elected to membership in the National Institute of Arts and Letters.

May Swenson is famous for using interesting wordplay and puzzling riddles in her poetry.

Sculptor Cyrus Dallin is best known for his sculptures of Native Americans, but he also created Salt Lake City's statue of Brigham Young and a statue of a Mormon angel that stands on top of the Salt Lake City Temple.

Utah's culture also includes a more modern-day view of art. The state boasts a number of artists from the performing arts—the big screen, little screen, and theater stage. One of the most famous of these artists is Donny Osmond, a singer, dancer, and actor who hails from Ogden. At age four Donny began singing and dancing professionally with his brothers as a member of the Osmond Family. The family appeared on many variety television shows in the 1960s. By the time Donny was a teenager, he had a number of hit records. He and his sister Marie also had their own television series from 1976 to 1979. More recently, Donny has starred in an international touring production of a musical play, and Marie has starred in another television series.

Beautiful music has had a long tradition in Utah. The Mormon Tabernacle Choir is one of the most respected groups of choral singers in the world. The 325-member choir has been performing weekly radio shows since 1929 and now also performs regularly on television. The choir has made hundreds of recordings while maintaining a standard of excellence that is recognized worldwide.

The Utah Symphony is also widely respected. The orchestra often accompanies the Mormon Tabernacle Choir in its recordings and performances. In addition, the Utah Opera Company stages several productions each year.

Utah also has many other performing arts companies. Modern and classical dance are regularly performed by companies such as Ballet West, the Ririe-Woodbury Dance Company, and the University of Utah's Repertory Dance Theater. The first theater playhouse west of the Mississippi River was built in Salt Lake City in 1852. The city has many fine theater companies, including Theatre Works West and Salt Lake Repertory Theatre, also known as "City Rep."

The people of Utah are proud of their state's exciting cultural diversity. They express this pride in their support of the Utah Arts Council, the oldest arts council in the nation. With the council's help, the culture of Utah is ensured preservation—and plenty of room for innovation—for years to come.

Actress Maude Adams is best known for her role as Peter Pan on Broadway. She starred in over 1,500 performances of the part, from 1905 to 1907.

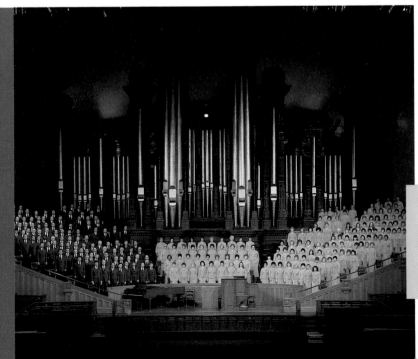

This photograph shows the Mormon Tabernacle Choir in front of the huge tabernacle organ. The organ's largest pipes are taller than thirty feet!

Utah: Arts Oasis in the Desert

Ask most people to list the things they could not live without, and they might mention food, water, shelter, or heat. A few might add art to their lists.

For Brigham Young and Utah's early Mormon settlers, the arts were among life's necessities. Mormon pioneers couldn't bring much with them in their journey west, but some made sure to pack pianos and other musical instruments. Young, who was known as a practical man, sent Utah artists to Europe to study. He also made sure a theater was built in Salt Lake City. Mormon pioneers began the choirs that eventually led to the formation of the world-famous Mormon Tabernacle Choir.

Why was art so important to the Mormon pioneers? They wanted to change the desert into a green and fertile farmland. The settlers worked hard to irrigate crops and built more than 150 self-sustaining towns by 1860. Art, especially music, helped them to keep up their spirits while they worked.

The Utah Arts Council's Folk Arts Program helps to preserve arts that reflect a traditional or ethnic culture, such as traditional food preparation. This man is grilling food for a festival at Zion National Park.

But Brigham Young had a more long-term goal in mind for the arts. He knew that to survive in a strange place, the settlers would have to work together. They would need to be reminded of their traditions and the history they had in common. Pulling a community together—sometimes stimulating it into action—has been a practical function of artists since the beginning of history.

Today, Brigham Young's dream of Utah as a community rich in art has become a reality. Thanks largely to the Utah Arts Council, Utah is often considered "an oasis of arts in the West."

The Utah Arts Institute, which is now the Utah Arts Council, was formed in 1899 by the third Utah state legislature. It is the oldest state arts agency in the nation. The Institute began by buying the work of visual artists, providing the artists with an income and the state with a collection of art.

Even during the troubled years of the Great Depression, Utah remained committed to its artists. Projects cosponsored by the Institute and the federal government provided jobs for artists at a time when any kind of work was hard to come by. Utah's writers produced a guide to Utah during the Depression, and musicians formed Utah's first civic orchestra. In 1965 the National Endowment for the Arts enabled the Utah Arts Council to expand its support for art.

Today, the Utah Arts Council can claim to have fulfilled its original goal to advance the arts and to encourage excellence among Utah's artists. Because the council believes that every individual has a right to artistic development, it brings artists into public schools and develops art classes for schools. The council still funds individual artists and writers with grants.

One of the arts supported by the Folk Arts Program of the Utah Arts Council is Native American weaving. Native Americans in the Southwest began weaving with cotton in A.D. 700.

37

The Utah Symphony is financed in part by a grant from the Utah Arts Endowment Fund of the Utah Arts Council.

Arts are an important part of maintaining cultural traditions, so the Utah Arts Council makes a point of sponsoring art from Utah's various cultures. The Folk Art program documents folk art and encourages people to become artists by buying works of art, sponsoring artists, and providing apprenticeships. Apprenticeships are opportunities for people to learn by doing. Folk artists can apply for apprenticeships in art forms such as quilting, Native American beadwork, Mexican *corridos* (songs that tell a story), and saddlemaking. By preserving folk art, the council also preserves the values of Utah's people.

Perhaps the most unusual accomplishment of the Utah Arts Council is its community-development program. Rural communities in Utah can bring performing artists into their community with money from the Utah Arts Council. Towns and organizations can ask the council for help developing the arts in their communities. They can also apply to the council for help in bringing art into building designs.

Utah is nineteenth in the nation in the amount of money it spends on art programs, not counting the grant money it gives directly to the Utah Symphony, Ballet West, and Utah Opera Company. The Utah Arts

Council is a part of the Utah Department of Community and Economic Development. That's because the people of Utah see art as an important part of their economy.

The arts are a small industry, bringing enormous economic benefits to Utah. In Salt Lake City alone, the state reaped $19 million in economic benefits from a state investment of less than $500,000. The arts contribute to a cultural environment in Utah that brings tourists, businesses, and other industries to the state. Brigham Young was a practical man, indeed, if he knew that pianos carted across the prairie in covered wagons would lead to all this.

The Utah Arts Council supports many dance companies, including companies that specialize in children's dance, ethnic dance, classical ballet, and modern dance.

He Knew What He Wanted

Throughout the history of the United States, people have moved to the West for a variety of reasons. For some, it was the promise of gold or the hope for religious freedom. For others, like Cecil Garland, it was simply the lure of the West itself.

Cecil Garland is a cattle rancher and hay farmer in a tiny Utah community called Caleo about seventy miles north of Great Basin National Park. He lives with his wife Annette and their daughter Bertha. Garland dreamed for many years of being a cowboy while he was growing up in North Carolina.

"When I was just maybe in high school," remembers Garland, "I knew that someday I was going to have a little ranch in the West somewhere. And Utah happened to be the place where I could find one . . . that was run-down enough to where I could afford it."

The ranch didn't stay run-down for long. Garland fixed it up, and has kept it running for about forty years. At age seventy, Garland is still actively ranching, living out the dreams of his youth.

Running a ranch isn't easy, however, especially in the dry Great Basin area of western Utah. As Garland said, "Most people come to this country and they look at it and say, 'What in the

The life of a Utah rancher is very isolated. Cecil Garland and his family have no doctor or supermarket in their town.

Parts of Utah are not ideally suited for anyone, except perhaps mountain men.

world does a cow eat here?'" But modern machinery and methods of irrigation have sprouted grass where no one believed it could grow.

Garland has taught his daughter these methods so that she will be able to keep the ranch running for many more years. Bertha is now learning even more at college, where she is studying for a degree in Animal Science. As Garland says, the ranchers of the area are eager to learn from their children. "The majority of ranchers of this country work hard to send their kids on to study animal science, range science, and soil science."

Although Cecil Garland maintains an open mind about new technology, he still has many traditional attitudes about life. These attitudes have served him well as he has forged an independent life in the difficult world of ranching. "I think the thing that we're losing, or have a tendency to forget in this country," Garland says, "[is that] with freedom comes a great personal responsibility. . . . And without that personal responsibility, that essential concern for welfare—not only of yourself, but of your neighbors and your country—then that freedom is lost."

Cecil Garland has learned many lessons over the years about farming and raising cattle. But it is the lessons of life that Garland brought with him to Utah that perhaps have made the attainment of his dream truly possible.

41

Looking Ahead from Day One

Utah is currently among the fastest-growing states in the country. Its economy is thriving, and it doesn't show signs of slowing down anytime soon.

Utah's future is dependent on the potential of its citizens. One reason Utah's future looks so good is because its citizens are among the best educated in the nation. Nearly 85 percent of Utah residents have finished high school. Utah has the second-highest percentage of high school graduates in the nation.

Much of the credit for Utah's success in education must go to the state government. The state has consistently placed in the top five for education spending in the first half of the 1990s. This means about forty percent of Utah's budget is spent on its students.

One issue that has caused debate concerns the protection of the environment. Utah's population growth has brought a need for expanding the amount of land the state currently allows for businesses and residents. Some industrialists also want to build in Utah's protected national parks and forests.

Utah's future depends on preserving its unprotected environment. Although the state has many national parks that are protected, these parks cover only 2.8 percent of the state.

The future is bright for Salt Lake City, Utah's capital and largest urban center. In 1990 *Fortune Magazine* named Salt Lake City the best city in the United States in which to locate a business.

Another issue related to the expanding population concerns the threat to the state's limited water supply. New industries especially have been depleting water sources—some factories can use more water in a day than a person uses in a lifetime! The dams and irrigation systems built by the Central Utah Project in 1967 are expected to provide enough water until 2020. The year 2020 no longer looks as far away as it did in the late 1960s, however.

One solution may be to limit the number of new businesses coming into the state. That may solve some concerns. But with so many new technologies being developed, the state risks turning away future big-money industries.

Utah has built a solid platform for the future with education and a strong economy. Whatever problems Utah faces in the years ahead, its citizens will be equipped to solve them.

Important Historical Events

400	The Anasazi arrive in present-day Utah.
900	The Fremont arrive in present-day Utah.
1300	The Anasazi and Fremont people break up into smaller groups.
1776	Spanish priests Francisco Atanasio Domínguez and Silvestre Vélez de Escalante explore the north-central Utah region.
1824	Mountain man Jim Bridger discovers Great Salt Lake.
1830	Joseph Smith founds the Church of Jesus Christ of Latter-day Saints in New York.
1842	John C. Frémont maps the Utah region.
1844	Joseph Smith is murdered.
1847	Brigham Young and a group of Mormon pioneers arrive at Great Salt Lake.
1848	Utah becomes an American territory when the United States wins the Mexican War.
1849	The Mormons organize the State of Deseret.
1850	Congress creates the Utah Territory.
1853	Ute leader Wakara attacks Mormon settlements.
1857	President James Buchanan sends federal troops to prevent a rumored rebellion. A group of Mormons join Native Americans in attacking a wagon train.
1858	Peace is made before any blood is shed in the Mormon War.
1861	The first transcontinental telegraph line stretches from California to Washington, D.C., after the two branches meet in Salt Lake City.

1865	The Black Hawk War begins.
1868	The last of the Ute are forced onto a reservation in northeastern Utah.
1869	The Union Pacific and Central Pacific railroads meet at Promontory, creating the nation's first transcontinental railroad.
1879	The United States Supreme Court upholds antipolygamy laws. Federal officers are sent to Utah to arrest Mormons who continue the practice.
1890	The Mormon church advises its members to give up polygamy.
1896	Utah is admitted to the Union as the forty-fifth state.
1918	Utah's mines, farms, and ranches fall into an economic slump.
1930	The Great Depression begins.
1938	The Mormon church begins construction of Welfare Square in Salt Lake City.
1942 to 1945	Over eight thousand people of Japanese descent are held in detention camps in Utah.
1952	Uranium is discovered in Utah.
1953	Utah passes the Water Pollution Control Act.
1954	The federal government terminates its recognition of the Utah Paiute.
1967	The Central Utah Project is started.
1980	Utah Paiute regain federal support.
1994	Utah's labor market ranks as "best in the nation."
1996	Utah celebrates the 100th anniversary of its admission to the United States.

Utah's flag displays the state coat of arms. The year of Utah's statehood is beneath the coat of arms. The coat of arms consists of an American eagle, six golden arrows, and two American flags surrounding a shield. The shield shows a beehive beneath the state motto. The state flower surrounds the beehive, and the year of the state's first American settlement is printed beneath the shield.

Utah Almanac

Nickname. The Beehive State

Capital. Salt Lake City

State Bird. Seagull

State Flower. Sego lily

State Tree. Blue spruce

State Motto. Industry

State Song. "Utah, We Love Thee"

State Abbreviations. Ut. (traditional); UT (postal)

Statehood. January 4, 1896, the 45th state

Government. Congress: U.S. senators, 2; U.S. representatives, 3. State Legislature: senators, 29; representatives, 75. Counties: 29

Area. 84,905 sq mi (219,902 sq km), 11th in size among the states

Greatest Distances. north/south, 342 mi (551 km); east/west, 276 mi (444 km)

Elevation. Highest: Kings Point, 13,528 ft (4,123 m). Lowest: 2,000 ft (610 m)

Population. 1990 Census: 1,727,784 (18% increase over 1980), 35th among the states. Density: 20 persons per sq mi (8 persons per sq km). Distribution: 87% urban, 13% rural. 1980 Census: 1,461,037

Economy. *Agriculture*: beef and dairy cattle, turkeys, sheep, hay, barley, pears, cherries, honey. *Manufacturing*: transportation equipment, food processing, computer software, biomedical products. *Mining*: oil, coal, copper, gold, silver, natural gas, lead, uranium

State Seal

State Flower: Sego lily

State Bird: Seagull

Annual Events

★ Hogsback Ridge Competitive Snowmobile Hill Climb in Wellsville (February)

★ Living Traditions Festival in Salt Lake City (May)

★ Paiute Restoration Gathering and Pow-wow in Cedar City (June)

★ Outlaw Trail Festival in Vernal (June/July)

★ Pioneer Days in Ogden (July)

★ Festival of the American West in Logan (July/August)

★ Southern Utah Folklife Festival in Zion National Park near Springdale (September)

★ Utah State Fair in Salt Lake City (September)

Places to Visit

★ Anasazi Indian Village State Park in Boulder

★ Beehive House in Salt Lake City

★ Bonneville Salt Flats and Speedway, near Wendover

★ Butch Cassidy's Family Cabin in Circleville

★ Dinosaur National Monument and Dinosaur Garden in Vernal

★ Earth Science Museum in Provo

★ Fremont Indian State Park, near Sevier

★ Golden Spike National Historic Site, near Brigham City

★ Hovenweep National Monument, near Blanding

★ Museum of Natural History in Salt Lake City

Index